(25p

Perfect Cooking

—WITH—

MUSTARD

Ayee Mendes da Costa

HAMLYN

Illustrations
by Simon Josebury

Published 1985 by
Hamlyn Publishing, a division of
The Hamlyn Publishing Group Ltd,
Bridge House, 69 London Road,
Twickenham, Middlesex

© Elvendon Press 1982, 1985

ISBN 0 600 32541 5

Printed in Italy

CONTENTS

INTRODUCTION

Mustard is a condiment which has been used since the Middle Ages. If you browse through the shelves of any supermarket or delicatessen now, there are countless varieties from which to choose, and it is easy to become confused. What actually is the difference between all those brands? If you read the labels, the lists of ingredients will invariably list mustard seed, vinegar and spices. Therein lies the answer. Each type of mustard makes use of different vinegars and spices. Many use wine instead of, or in addition to, the vinegar. Some use whole mustard seeds, others use ground. Some use a combination of whole and ground. And the combinations of spices are infinite.

All of these recipes have been kitchen tested and will succeed with any mustard you choose. The differences in taste will show up most clearly in the strength of the mustard and the amount of salt it contains. Most mustards do not need much extra seasoning, but do taste your dishes and decide for yourself.

Mrs. da Costa uses mustard as a seasoning. This does not mean that any food seasoned with mustard tastes of nothing but mustard. Far from it. As with all spices, mustard can be used to enhance the natural flavour of your other ingredients. When used in large quantities to coat your meat or fish, or to season a sauce, it does of course alter the flavour but in such a way that the results will draw nothing but compliments.

When submitting this manuscript, Mrs. da Costa wrote, "Mustard seed and mustard can be used in a variety of ways, but especially in all

kinds of pickles and marinades, and comple-
ments particularly the following: cheese dishes
and sauces, butters, fish, pork, veal, poultry as
well as red meat and game." Her own words
cover almost the entire range of cookery. There
is little left out, and the range of recipes presented
in this book should set you well on the way to
Perfect Cooking with MUSTARD.

Bernice Hurst

QUICK MUSTARD SAUCE		
Metric		*Imperial*
2 x 15 ml sp	butter	2 tbsp
½ x 15 ml sp	mustard	½ tbsp
few drops	lemon juice	few drops
250 ml	yoghurt *OR*	8 oz
single cream *OR* soured cream		

Combine the butter, mustard and lemon juice. Mix well with a fork. (The mustard butter can be prepared in larger quantities and kept refrigerated for several days.) Add the yoghurt or cream, and mix well. This sauce does not need to be cooked—simply pour it over your favourite roast meat before serving.

CHEESE SAUCE		
Metric		*Imperial*
1 x 15 ml sp	butter	1 tbsp
¼ x 15 ml sp	mustard	¼ tbsp
few drops	lemon juice	few drops
1 x 15 ml sp	rice flour	1 tbsp
575 ml	milk	1 pint
125 g	grated cheese	4 oz

Combine the butter, mustard and lemon juice. Mix well with a fork. (The mustard butter can be prepared in larger quantities and kept refrigerated for several days.) Thoroughly combine the mustard butter and rice flour. Add to the milk and bring to the boil. Add the cheese and stir until it has melted.

BLUE CHEESE SAUCE

Metric		Imperial
1 x 15 ml sp	mustard	1 tbsp
1 x 15 ml sp	Bresse-Bleu cheese	1 tbsp
2–3	chopped tomatoes	2–3
	salt and pepper	

Work the mustard and cheese together with a fork until the mixture is soft and smooth. Stir in the tomatoes. Season to taste with salt and pepper. Chill and serve with cold fish dishes.

BARBECUE SAUCE

Metric		Imperial
1 x 15 ml sp	mustard	1 tbsp
2	cloves garlic	2
1 x 5 ml sp	chives	1 tsp
1 x 5 ml sp	tarragon	1 tsp
few drops	lemon juice	few drops

Finely chop the garlic and herbs. Stir into the mustard. Add the lemon juice and mix well. This sauce is especially delicious when used for prawns. The sauce should be spread over the prawns or your other barbecue ingredients just before you are ready to start cooking.

AVOCADO MAYONNAISE

Metric		Imperial
1	medium avocado	1
1	large egg	1
1	lemon	1
3 x 15 ml sp	oil	3 tbsp
1 x 5 ml sp	mustard	1 tsp

Remove the avocado from its skin. Chop the flesh roughly and place in a liquidiser. Squeeze the juice from the lemon and add to the liquidiser along with the egg, oil and mustard. Blend until smooth and creamy. Transfer to a container, cover and refrigerate until ready to serve. This dressing is an excellent complement for chicken, fish or any vegetable salad.

SOURED CREAM DRESSING

Metric		Imperial
1 x 15 ml sp	wine vinegar	1 tbsp
1 x 15 ml sp	mustard	1 tbsp
300 ml	soured cream	1 cup

Thoroughly mix together all the dressing ingredients, and serve with your favourite salad. As a variation, substitute lemon juice for the vinegar.

MUSHROOM SOUP

Metric		Imperial
225 g	mushrooms	8 oz
50 g	butter	2 oz
300 ml	stock	½ pint
4 x 15 ml sp	cream	4 tbsp
2 x 15 ml sp	sherry	2 tbsp
1 x 15 ml sp	mustard	1 tbsp

Chop the mushrooms and soften in the melted butter. Stir in the stock, sherry and mustard. Bring to the boil, then lower the heat and simmer very gently for 15 minutes. Cool and liquidise. Reheat and, just before serving, stir in the cream.

BREAD SOUP

Metric		Imperial
	stale bread	
125 g	grated cheese	4 oz
½–1 litre	stock	1–2 pints
1 x 15 ml sp	mustard	1 tbsp

Bring the stock and mustard to boiling point. Crumble the stale bread and grated cheese into a tureen. Pour over the stock and serve immediately. (*Note*—the amount of bread required depends on the amount of stock used, and the thickness of soup intended.)

VEGETABLES AU GRATIN

Metric		Imperial
900 g	vegetables	2 lb
few drops	lemon juice	few drops
25 g	butter	1 oz
1 x 15 ml sp	rice flour	1 tbsp
125 g	grated cheese	4 oz
1 x 15 ml sp	mustard	1 tbsp
pinch	nutmeg	pinch
250 ml	single cream OR soured cream	8 oz

Melt half of the butter, add the lemon juice, and gently fry the vegetables until they are soft. Drain and remove, reserving the pan juices. The most suitable vegetables to use are chicory, courgettes or artichoke hearts.

To prepare the sauce, combine the remaining pan juices, butter, lemon juice and rice flour. Stir into the single or soured cream. Arrange the vegetables in an ovenproof dish and pour over the sauce. Combine the grated cheese and mustard. Sprinkle over the sauce. Bake 15 minutes at No. 6 (400). Serve immediately.

ROQUEFORT TERRINE

Metric		Imperial
300 g	**Roquefort** OR **Blue Stilton**	12 oz
250 g	chopped walnuts	10 oz
150 g	butter	6 oz
2 x 15 ml sp	brandy	2 tbsp
1 x 15 ml sp	mustard	1 tbsp
1 x 15 ml sp	chives OR chervil	1 tbsp

Soften the cheese and place in a liquidiser with all the other ingredients. Blend until smooth and creamy. Transfer to a dish, cover and chill until ready to serve.

The terrine can be served sliced with toast or biscuits, but is equally delicious when used to fill stalks of celery, or peach or avocado halves.

Roquefort Terrine

ROQUEFORT TART

Metric		Imperial
100 g	Roquefort	3 oz
75 ml	single cream	3 oz
1 x 15 ml sp	mustard	1 tbsp
2	eggs	2
100 g	chopped walnuts	3 oz

Soften the cheese, beat in the eggs, and combine with the other ingredients. Pour into a 9in. pie dish or quiche tin. Bake in a medium oven until golden.

CARROT LOAF

Metric		Imperial
900 g	cooked carrots	2 lb
3	eggs	3
1 x 15 ml sp	mustard	1 tsp
	salt and pepper	

Line a loaf pan with shortcrust pastry. Combine the cooked, mashed carrots with beaten eggs. Season to taste with mustard, salt and pepper. Turn into the pan and bake until the filling has set. Turn out and serve with a bechamel sauce.

CHEESE SOUFFLÉ

Metric		Imperial
3	**eggs**	3
25 g	**rice flour**	1 oz
1 x 15 ml sp	**mustard**	1 tbsp
125 g	**grated cheese**	4 oz
300 ml	**milk**	½ pint

Separate the eggs. Beat the whites until they are stiff but not dry. Combine the rice flour and mustard. Stir in the egg yolks, then the milk and cheese. Mix well. Gently fold in the egg whites, starting with just one spoonful in order to loosen the mixture. Turn into an oiled soufflé dish and bake for 30 minutes at No. 5 (375). Serve immediately.

For a more exotic soufflé, stir any of the following into the egg yolk mixture:

2 x 15 ml sp	sweetcorn *OR*	2 tbsp
	chopped ham *OR*	
	cooked bacon *OR*	
	tuna fish *OR*	
	cooked mushrooms	

CHEESE PUFFS

Metric		Imperial
450 g	puff pastry	1 lb
2 x 15 ml sp	butter	2 tbsp
½ x 15 ml sp	mustard	½ tbsp
few drops	lemon juice	few drops
125 g	blue cheese	4 oz
	nutmeg	
	sesame seeds	
	milk	

Roll the pastry out thinly to a large rectangle. Combine the butter, mustard and lemon juice. Mix well with a fork. Spread the mustard butter evenly but sparingly down the centre. Crumble the cheese over the butter. Sprinkle with nutmeg. Fold one side of the pastry into the middle, brush with milk and then fold the other side on top so they overlap slightly in the middle. Press the ends down gently. Place seam side down on a baking tray. Brush the entire surface with milk and sprinkle sesame seeds on top. Bake for 15–20 minutes at No. 6 (400).

As an alternative to blue cheese, use Cheddar or Gruyère, and spread the contents of a small package of defrosted chopped spinach over the filling before sealing.

To make individual servings, before baking cut across the roll at 3 inch intervals.

AUBERGINE DIP

Metric		Imperial
2	large aubergines	2
1	clove garlic	1
1	lemon	1
1 x 15 ml sp	mustard	1 tbsp
	chopped parsley	

Bake the aubergines until the skin is dark and wrinkled and the flesh is soft. Cool under the tap and split in half. Scoop out the flesh and place it in the liquidiser along with the garlic, mustard and the juice from the lemon. Blend until smooth. Transfer to a serving dish, cover and chill. Garnish with chopped parsley.

EGGS WITH MUSTARD SAUCE

Metric		Imperial
6	hard boiled eggs	6
25 g	butter	1 oz
2 x 15 ml sp	cream	2 tbsp
1 x 15 ml sp	mustard	1 tbsp
125 g	prawns	4 oz
1 x 15 ml sp	chopped parsley	1 tbsp

Shell the eggs, slice in half and arrange in a serving dish. Warm the cream, butter, mustard, parsley and prawns. Pour over the eggs and serve.

EGGS WITH CIDER

Metric		Imperial
9	hard boiled eggs	9
675 g	onions	1½ lb
50 g	butter	2 oz
3 x 15 ml sp	mustard	3 tbsp
25 g	cornflour	1 oz
125 ml	soured cream	4 oz
1 x 15 ml sp	chives	1 tbsp
1 x 15 ml sp	parsley	1 tbsp
575 ml	cider	1 pint

Finely chop the onions and cook gently in the melted butter until they are soft and golden. Stir in the cornflour, and cook for 1 minute. Slowly add the cider, stirring constantly. Continue to cook, still stirring, for 10 minutes. Do not allow the sauce to boil. Combine the soured cream and mustard. Add to the sauce.

Cut the eggs in half and arrange in a serving dish. Pour the sauce over the eggs and garnish with chopped chives and parsley. This dish should be served immediately after the eggs have been cooked, while they are still hot.

BAKED TROUT

Metric		Imperial
2	trout	2
2 x 15 ml sp	butter	2 tbsp
½ x 15 ml sp	mustard	½ tbsp
few drops	lemon juice	few drops

Combine the butter, mustard and lemon juice. Mix well with a fork. Clean the trout and place a spoonful of mustard butter in each. Add a few drops of lemon juice. Wrap loosely in tin foil. Place in an ovenproof dish and bake 25–30 minutes at No. 5 (375).

BAKED FISH FILLETS

Metric		Imperial
450 g	fish fillets	1 lb
450 g	frozen spinach	1 lb
250 ml	soured cream	8 oz
1 x 15 ml sp	mustard	1 tbsp
75 g	grated cheese	3 oz
	nutmeg	

Defrost the spinach and arrange on the bottom of a buttered ovenproof dish. Place the fish on top. Combine the soured cream and mustard. Pour over the fish. Top with the grated cheese and sprinkle with nutmeg. Bake 30 minutes at No. 4 (350).

MARINATED FISH		
Metric		*Imperial*
900 g	**fish**	2 lb
	oil	
	lemon juice	
	salt and pepper	
	thyme	
	parsley	
2	**hard boiled eggs**	2
2	**glasses white wine**	2
3	**chopped shallots** *OR*	3
2 x 15 ml sp	**chopped onion**	2 tbsp
1 x 15 ml sp	**mustard**	1 tbsp

The fish for this dish can be bream, plaice, sole or trout. Combine the oil, lemon juice, seasoning and herbs. Clean the fish and marinate for several hours (or overnight if possible). Grill and serve accompanied by the sauce.

To make the sauce, pour the wine into a saucepan with the shallots or onions, and boil until it has reduced. Add the mustard and the mashed yolks of the hardboiled eggs. Heat through. Season and stir in some chopped parsley. Serve with the fish.

Marinated Fi

CHICKEN WITH CREAM SAUCE

Metric		Imperial
1.5 kg	chicken	3–3½ lb
5 x 15 ml sp	olive oil	5 tbsp
2	cloves garlic	2
6 x 15 ml sp	wine vinegar	7 tbsp
1	glass white wine	1
2 x 15 ml sp	mustard	2 tbsp
1 x 15 ml sp	tomato purée	1 tbsp
4 x 15 ml sp	cream	4 tbsp
	chervil	
	parsley	

Cut the chicken into 4–8 serving pieces and brown, with the garlic cloves, in the heated olive oil. Cover and cook for 20 minutes. Add the wine vinegar, bring to the boil and allow to reduce to ¼. Remove the chicken pieces, and keep them warm.

Add the wine, mustard and tomato purée to the pan juices. Stir well and cook for 5 minutes. Remove the garlic cloves and stir in the cream. Do not allow the sauce to boil.

Arrange the chicken pieces on a serving dish. Pour over the sauce. Garnish with chervil and parsley. Serve immediately.

CHICKEN WITH CHEESE SAUCE

Metric		Imperial
1.5 kg	chicken	3–3½ lb
450 g	onions	1 lb
900 g	potatoes	2 lb
1 x 15 ml sp	mustard	1 tbsp
1 x 15 ml sp	rice flour	1 tbsp
	nutmeg	
	grated cheese	

Steam the chicken, potatoes and onions for 30 minutes. Remove, and when the chicken has cooled, cut it into serving pieces. Remove the skin, wing tips and other bony portions. Return these to the liquid in the cooking pan and simmer for another 45 minutes. Place an ice cube in the stock and remove once the fat has clung to it but before it has time to melt.

Arrange the chicken pieces, potatoes and onions in an ovenproof dish. The potatoes and onions can be left whole or sliced at this stage.

To make the sauce, melt the butter in a saucepan. Stir in the rice flour and mustard. Cook for 1 minute. Add the stock slowly, stirring constantly, until the pan contains about 1 pint (575 ml) of sauce. Bring to the boil and add more stock if the sauce seems too thick. Season with nutmeg. Pour the sauce over the chicken and sprinkle grated cheese on top—the amount required depends on individual tastes. Bake the dish for 30 minutes, or until it is golden brown, at No. 4 (350).

RABBIT WITH MUSTARD SAUCE

Metric		Imperial
900 g	rabbit	2 lb
	salt	
	mustard	
2 x 15 ml sp	oil	2 tbsp
1 x 15 ml sp	mixed herbs	1 tbsp
2	glasses white wine	2

Cut the rabbit into serving portions and sprinkle with salt. Leave for 10 minutes, then coat the meat with mustard on all sides. Leave for 30 minutes.

Heat the oil in a heavy bottomed saucepan. Sauté the meat until it is golden on all sides. It will need to be turned constantly. Add the herbs and stir for 2–3 minutes longer. Remove the meat from the pan, but keep warm. Stir the wine into the pan juices and heat through. Arrange the rabbit in a serving dish, pour over the sauce and serve immediately.

VEAL IN WHITE WINE

Metric		Imperial
900 g	veal	2 lb
125 g	belly pork	4 oz
	oil	
3	cloves garlic	3
2 x 15 ml sp	mustard	2 tbsp
1	tomato	1
1	glass white wine	1
3 x 15 ml sp	chopped parsley	3 tbsp

Cut the veal and pork into small pieces. Brown them in the hot oil. Add the mustard, chopped garlic, tomato and parsley, and the glass of white wine. Mix well. Cover the pan and simmer gently for 30 minutes. Garnish with more parsley and serve.

This dish is equally successful when rabbit is substituted for veal.

Veal in
white wine

MEATLOAF

Metric		Imperial
450 g	minced meat	1 lb
250 ml	yoghurt OR soured cream	8 oz
2 x 15 ml sp	mustard	2 tbsp
1	glass dry vermouth	1
1	loaf crusty bread	1
1–2	eggs	1–2

Slice the top off the loaf of bread and remove the soft inside. Crumble the inside and sprinkle on an ovenproof tray. Place in the oven to dry out for 30 minutes at No. 4 (350).

For the meat, use either lamb or beef. Mix in with the yoghurt or soured cream (or a mixture of both), the mustard and vermouth. Add the dry crumbs. Mix well. Pack the meat mixture into the bread shell. Put the top back on the loaf. Brush the bread with melted butter (mustard flavoured if you have some), and bake for 30 minutes at No. 6 (400).

BEEF STEW WITH BEETROOT

Metric		Imperial
675 g	stewing beef	1½ lb
4	onions	4
1 x 15 ml sp	mustard	1 tbsp
1	bay leaf	1
	boiled beetroot	
	boiled potatoes	

Cut the beef into small pieces. Steam the beef, 1 onion and the bay leaf for 50 minutes. Remove the meat. In the juices cook the remaining chopped onions. Add the meat again, some small beetroot, a few potatoes and the mustard. Stir well and mash a potato and a piece of beetroot to thicken the sauce. The number of potatoes and pieces of beetroot used must be left to individual taste.

When serving the stew, add a small pickled cucumber and a hard boiled egg to each person's portion.

Beef Stew with beetroot

LAMB WITH AUBERGINES

Metric		Imperial
450 g	lamb	1 lb
225 g	bacon	½ lb
2	medium aubergines	2
1 x 15 ml sp	mustard	1 tbsp
150 ml	olive oil	¼ pint
1	lemon	1
12	small onions	12
	mixed herbs *e.g.* **tarragon, parsley, chervil, thyme**	

Cut the lamb into small cubes. Combine the olive oil, juice and grated rind of the lemon, and the herbs. Marinate the meat for several hours (or overnight if possible), turning occasionally. Approximately 1 hour after putting the meat into the marinade, add the aubergines, bacon and onions. The aubergines should be peeled and sliced, the bacon cut into cubes. If small onions are not available, use larger ones and cut them into quarters.

When you are ready to begin cooking, thread pieces of lamb, bacon, aubergine and onion onto skewers. Grill for 10–12 minutes, turning occasionally.

BAKED PORK

Metric		Imperial
4	pork chops *OR* pork steaks	4
1	onion	1
1	clove garlic	1
2 x 15 ml sp	oil	2 tbsp
125 g	grated cheese	4 oz
1 x 15 ml sp	mustard	1 tbsp
50 g	mushrooms	2 oz
125 ml	cream *OR* soured cream	4 oz
	nutmeg	

Finely chop the onion and garlic. Sauté gently in the heated oil until they are soft. Add the pork chops or steaks (or lamb chops if you prefer), and brown quickly on both sides. Remove the meat from the pan and place in an ovenproof dish which has been generously lined with tin foil. The foil will be folded over to enclose the meat for cooking, so ensure that it is large enough for this. Arrange the onions on top of the meat. Combine the cream, cheese, mustard, mushrooms and nutmeg. Pour over the meat. Fold the tin foil to seal the meat in and bake for 30 minutes at No. 2 (300).

DEVILLED KIDNEYS

Metric		Imperial
4	kidneys	4
1 x 15 ml sp	butter	1 tbsp
4	shallots *OR*	4
1	small onion	1
1	liqueur glass brandy	1
1 x 15 ml sp	mustard	1 tbsp
300 ml	cream	10 oz
	chervil	

Cut the kidneys into halves and remove the
nerves and fat. Cut into bite size pieces. Melt the
butter. Quickly fry the kidneys. Remove and
keep warm. Sauté the finely chopped shallots or
onion in the pan juices. Add the brandy and
reduce. Stir in the mustard and cream, then
return the kidney pieces to the pan and mix well.
Sprinkle in the chervil and cook, stirring
constantly, for 5–10 minutes.

LIVER WITH ORANGE

Metric		Imperial
675 g	calf's liver	1½ lb
2 x 15 ml sp	oil	2 tbsp
1 x 15 ml sp	mustard	1 tbsp
2	cloves garlic	2
1	onion	1
1	glass red wine	1
1	orange	1
	parsley	
	thyme	

Quickly fry the slices of liver in the heated oil for 3 minutes. Transfer to an ovenproof dish. Fry the finely chopped onion and crushed garlic in the pan juices until they are brown. Add the wine, mustard and herbs. Simmer for 5 minutes. Pour the sauce over the liver. Garnish with thinly sliced orange.

Liver with Orange

LEMON CHUTNEY

Metric		Imperial
450 g	onions	1 lb
5	large lemons	5
575 ml	wine vinegar	1 pint
50 g	mustard seeds	2 oz
450 g	sugar	1 lb
1 x 5 ml sp	allspice	1 tsp
125 g	seedless raisins	4 oz

Wash the lemons and cut into pieces, removing all the pips. Sprinkle with salt and leave overnight.

Put all the ingredients into a heavy bottomed saucepan. Add a knob of butter to prevent the chutney boiling over and bring to the boil. Simmer for 45 minutes. Spoon into warmed jars and seal.

Lemon Chutney

APPLE AND RAISIN CHUTNEY

Metric		Imperial
2025 g	apples	4½ lb
675 g	raisins	1½ lb
575 ml	vinegar	1 pint
450 g	sugar	1 lb
125 g	salt	4 oz
50 g	mustard seeds	2 oz
25 g	powdered ginger	1 oz
3	cloves garlic	3
1	cinnamon stick	1

Peel and chop the apples, removing all the pips. Place in a heavy bottomed saucepan along with the sultanas, vinegar, sugar and garlic. Add a knob of butter to prevent the chutney boiling over. Bring to the boil and simmer for 45 minutes. Add the remaining ingredients and simmer for 10 minutes longer. Leave loosely covered overnight. The next day, bring to the boil once more and cook for 7 minutes. Spoon into warmed jars and seal.